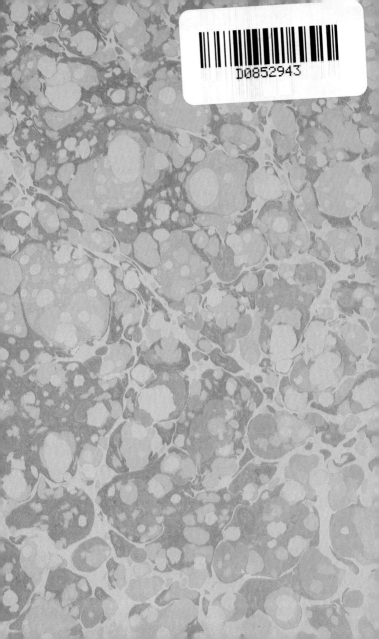

GREAT AMERICAN POETS

GREAT AMERICAN POETS

Emily Dickinson

Edited and with an introduction
by Geoffrey Moore

Clarkson N. Potter, Inc./Publishers NEW YORK
DISTRIBUTED BY CROWN PUBLISHERS, INC.

Selection and Introduction copyright © 1986 by Geoffrey Moore

Published in the United States by Clarkson N. Potter, Inc.,
225 Park Avenue South, New York, New York 10003
and represented in Canada by the Canadian MANDA group
Published in Great Britain by Aurum Press Ltd.,
33 Museum Street, London WC1A 1LD, England

CLARKSON N. POTTER, POTTER, THE GREAT POETS,
and colophon are trademarks of Clarkson N. Potter, Inc.

Picture research by Juliet Brightmore

Manufactured in Hong Kong

Library of Congress Cataloging-in-Publication Data
Dickinson, Emily, 1830–1886.
    Great American poets.
        I. Title.
    PS1541.A6 1986 811′.4 86-5039
    ISBN 0-517-56290-1

10 9 8 7 6 5 4 3 2

First Edition

CONTENTS

INTRODUCTION

Emily Dickinson was born in Amherst, Massachusetts, in 1830 and died there in 1886. The family was a distinguished one: Emily's grandfather had founded Amherst College, and her father was a lawyer and State Congressman. Emily herself was renowned for her wit in a lively and sociable household – until her middle twenties. From that time on she became a recluse.

Speculation has it that the reason was unrequited love. Emily's niece, Martha Dickinson (Bianchi), said that she 'met her fate' in the person of a renowned Philadelphia preacher. This can only have been the Reverend Charles Wadsworth, with whom we know for certain she cultivated an 'intellectual friendship'. Other names, and reasons, have been advanced for Emily's self-imposed retirement.

What is important to us, however, is her poetry. This did not come to light until after her death, when her sister Lavinia handed over some of Emily's papers to 'Sister Sue', her brother's wife. Sue entrusted the work of editing to Professor and Mrs Todd of Amherst College. From the approximately 700 poems then discovered, Mrs Todd (with the help of Thomas Wentworth Higginson) brought out the *First Series* of Emily's poems in 1890. Two more *Series* appeared, in 1891 and 1896, all considerably doctored by the correct and somewhat embarrassed Higginson. More poems, under the title of *The Single Hound*, came out in 1914, edited by Martha Dickinson Bianchi. *Further Poems* by Mrs Bianchi and Alfred Leete Hampson was published in 1929, and the first collected volume, *The Poems of Emily Dickinson*, by the same editors, appeared in 1937.

It was known for many years that this text, like the Todd–Higginson ones, was by no means accurate; but friends and relatives kept the manuscripts jealously guarded until the 1950s, when Thomas H. Johnson of the Lawrenceville School, New Jersey, was allowed to see all the manuscripts. In 1955 he published his three-volume variorum edition of *The Poems of Emily Dickinson* and it was revealed that the actual number of Emily's poems stood at 1775. In 1960 Mr Johnson made a one-volume edition, and it is from this that the present selection was made.*

On 15 April 1862, when Emily was thirty-one years old, she had written to Higginson, a well-known New England 'man of letters', enclosing four of her poems. She wished to know whether her verses 'breathed'. We do not have his reply but we have Emily's side of the correspondence. 'You think,' she says, 'my gait "spasmodic". I am in no danger, Sir. You think me "uncontrolled". I have no Tribunal . . . The Sailor cannot see the North, but knows the Needle can.'

So much for Higginson – put firmly in his place. Emily Dickinson knew herself a true poet and she did not need contemporary endorsement. Indeed, the poems of the sixties are much concerned with 'fame', as if she were anticipating what was to come after her death. Like most good poets, she expressed herself

Publisher's note. It is regretted that, for copyright reasons, the Harvard variorum edition from which Geoffrey Moore made his selection could not be used, and it is the earlier versions of the poems which are printed here. The discrepancies between what Emily Dickinson wrote and the 'improvements' made by her nineteenth-century editors are listed on p. 59.

more frequently through metaphor then simile, and her metaphors first make the reader pause at their strangeness – and then agree to their justness. Contemporary as she was with the late-Romantic Victorians, she could not avoid a certain amount of whimsicality; but this is very small. 'I like to see it lap the miles': on the face of it an ecstatic young lady's cry, yields, at a closer look, an odd and typical ambiguity. Her metaphors, 'gazing grain', 'zero at the bone', are as penetrating as her irony ('Because I could not stop for Death, He kindly stopped for me'), which reaches the point of paradox in 'Parting is all we know of heaven/ And all we need of hell.'

Her persistent use of Common Metre and the hymn-like, nursery rhyme-like regularity of her stanza must be set against the grimness of her images, her dramatic shifts of tone and the truly metaphysical cast of her imagination. Emily Dickinson had the power and perception of a great poet. Unfortunately her professional skill did not match her poetic vision – a fact of which she may well have been aware. Unwilling, therefore, to subvert this vision to her comparatively poor craft, we might speculate that she 'let herself go'. The result is the extraordinary combination of unorthodoxy and accuracy which we find in Emily's poems: a unique combination of prosodic idiosyncracy and moral insight. Through the power of her imagination she transformed her personal experience into universal truth. After Whitman – so different in style yet so similar in his independence – Emily Dickinson is the most important American poet of the nineteenth century.

GEOFFREY MOORE

Exultation is the going
Of an inland soul to sea,—
Past the houses, past the headlands,
Into deep eternity!

Bred as we, among the mountains,
Can the sailor understand
The divine intoxication
Of the first league out from land?

❧❧❧

I never hear the word 'escape'
Without a quicker blood,
A sudden expectation,
A flying attitude.

I never hear of prisons broad
By soldiers battered down,
But I tug childish at my bars,—
Only to fail again!

Success is counted sweetest
By those who ne'er succeed.
To comprehend a nectar
Requires sorest need.

Not one of all the purple Host
Who took the flag to-day
Can tell the definition,
So clear, of victory,

As he, defeated, dying,
On whose forbidden ear
The distant strains of triumph
Break agonized and clear.

Some things that fly there be,—
Birds, hours, the bumble-bee:
Of these no elegy.

Some things that stay there be,—
Grief, hills, eternity:
Nor this behooveth me.

There are, that resting, rise.
Can I expound the skies?
How still the riddle lies!

To fight aloud is very brave,
But gallanter, I know,
Who charge within the bosom,
The cavalry of woe.

Who win, and nations do not see,
Who fall, and none observe,
Whose dying eyes no country
Regards with patriot love.

We trust, in plumed procession,
For such the angels go,
Rank after rank, with even feet
And uniforms of snow.

An altered look about the hills;
A Tyrian light the village fills;
A wider sunrise in the dawn;
A deeper twilight on the lawn;
A print of a vermillion foot;
A purple finger on the slope;
A flippant fly upon the pane;
A spider at his trade again;
An added strut in chanticleer;
A flower expected everywhere;
An axe shrill singing in the woods;
Fern-odors on untravelled roads,
All this, and more I cannot tell,
A furtive look you know as well,
And Nicodemus' mystery
Receives its annual reply.

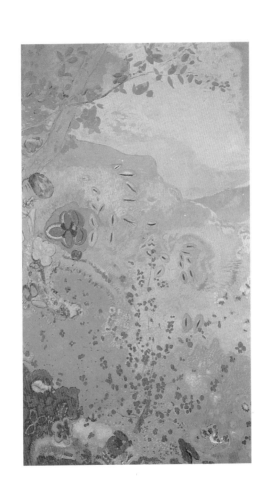

I taste a liquor never brewed,
From tankards scooped in pearl;
Not all the vats upon the Rhine
Yield such an alcohol!

Inebriate of air am I,
And debauchee of dew,
Reeling, through endless summer days,
From inns of molten blue.

When landlords turn the drunken bee
Out of the foxglove's door,
When butterflies renounce their drams,
I shall but drink the more!

Till seraphs swing their snowy hats,
And saints to windows run,
To see the little tippler
Leaning against the sun!

Safe in their alabaster chambers,
Untouched by morning and untouched by noon,
Sleep the meek members of the resurrection,
Rafter of satin, and roof of stone.

Light laughs the breeze in her castle of sunshine,
Babbles the bee in a stolid ear;
Pipe the sweet birds in ignorant cadence,
Ah, what sagacity perished here!

Grand go the years in the crescent above them;
Worlds scoop their arcs, and firmaments row,
Diadems drop and Doges surrender,
Soundless as dots on a disk of snow.

Hope is the thing with feathers
That perches in the soul,
And sings the tune without the words,
And never stops at all,

And sweetest in the gale is heard;
And sore must be the storm
That could abash the little bird
That kept so many warm.

I've heard it in the chillest land,
And on the strangest sea;
Yet, never, in extremity,
It asked a crumb of me.

I like a look of agony,
Because I know it's true;
Men do not sham convulsion,
Nor simulate a throe.

The eyes glaze once, and that is death.
Impossible to feign
The beads upon the forehead
By homely anguish strung.

I'm nobody! Who are you?
Are you nobody, too?
Then there's a pair of us—don't tell!
They'd banish us, you know.

How dreary to be somebody!
How public, like a frog
To tell your name the livelong day
To an admiring bog!

I felt a funeral in my brain,
And mourners, to and fro,
Kept treading, treading, till it seemed
That sense was breaking through.

And when they all were seated,
A service like a drum
Kept beating, beating, till I thought
My mind was going numb.

And then I heard them lift a box,
And creak across my soul
With those same boots of lead, again.
Then space began to toll

As all the heavens were a bell,
And being but an ear,
And I and silence some strange race,
Wrecked, solitary, here.

There's a certain slant of light,
On winter afternoons,
That oppresses, like the weight
Of cathedral tunes.

Heavenly hurt it gives us;
We can find no scar,
But internal difference,
Where the meanings are.

None may teach it anything,
'T is the seal, despair, —
An imperial affliction
Sent us of the air.

When it comes, the landscape listens,
Shadows hold their breath;
When it goes, 't is like the distance
On the look of death.

The soul selects her own society,
Then shuts the door;
On her divine majority
Obtrude no more.

Unmoved, she notes the chariot's pausing
At her low gate;
Unmoved, an emperor be kneeling
Upon her mat.

I've known her from an ample nation
Choose one;
Then close the valves of her attention
Like stone.

Some keep the Sabbath going to church;
I keep it staying at home,
With a bobolink for a chorister,
And an orchard for a dome.

Some keep the Sabbath in surplice,
I just wear my wings,
And instead of tolling the bell for church
Our little sexton sings.

God preaches,—a noted clergyman,—
And the sermon is never long;
So instead of getting to heaven at last,
I'm going all along!

I'll tell you how the sun rose,
A ribbon at a time.
The steeples swam in amethyst,
The news like squirrels ran.

The hills untied their bonnets,
The bobolinks begun.
Then I said softly to myself,
'That must have been the sun!'

.   .   .   .

But how he set, I know not.
There seemed a purple stile
That little yellow boys and girls
Were climbing all the while

Till when they reached the other side,
A dominie in gray
Put gently up the evening bars,
And led the flock away.

What soft, cherubic creatures
These gentlewomen are!
One would as soon assault a plush
Or violate a star.

Such dimity convictions,
A horror so refined
Of freckled human nature,
Of Deity ashamed,

It's such a common glory,
A fisherman's degree!
Redemption, brittle lady,
Be so, ashamed of thee.

I heard a fly buzz when I died;
The stillness round my form
Was like the stillness in the air
Between the heaves of storm.

The eyes beside had wrung them dry,
And breaths were gathering sure
For that last onset, when the king
Be witnessed in his power.

I willed my keepsakes, signed away
What portion of me I
Could make assignable, and then
There interposed a fly,

With blue, uncertain stumbling buzz,
Between the light and me;
And then the windows failed, and then
I could not see to see.

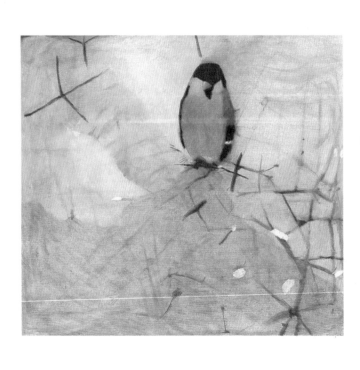

A bird came down the walk;
He did no know I saw;
He bit an angle-worm in halves
And ate the fellow, raw.

And then he drank a dew
From a convenient grass,
And then hopped sidewise to the wall
To let a beetle pass.

He glanced with rapid eyes
That hurried all abroad,—
They looked like frightened beads, I thought;
He stirred his velvet head

Like one in danger; cautious,
I offered him a crumb,
And he unrolled his feathers
And rowed him softer home

Than oars divide the ocean,
Too silver for a seam,
Or butterflies, off banks of noon,
Leap, plashless, as they swim.

I died for beauty, but was scarce
Adjusted in the tomb,
When one who died for truth was lain
In an adjoining room.

He questioned softly why I failed?
'For beauty,' I replied.
'And I for truth,–the two are one;
We brethren, are,' he said.

And so, as kinsmen, met a night,
We talked between the rooms,
Until the moss had reached our lips,
And covered up our names.

Much madness is divinest sense
To a discerning eye;
Much sense the starkest madness.
'T is the majority
In this, as all, prevails.
Assent, and you are sane;
Demur, you're straightway dangerous,
And handled with a chain.

The heart asks pleasure first,
And then, excuse from pain;
And then, those little anodynes
That deaden suffering;

And then, to go to sleep;
And then, if it should be
The will of its Inquisitor,
The liberty to die.

It was not death, for I stood up,
And all the dead lie down;
It was not night, for all the bells
Put out their tongues, for noon.

It was not frost, for on my flesh
I felt siroccos crawl,
Nor fire, for just my marble feet
Could keep a chancel cool.

And yet it tasted like them all;
The figures I have seen
Set orderly, for burial,
Reminded me of mine,

As if my life were shaven
And fitted to a frame,
And could not breathe without a key;
And 't was like midnight, some,

When everything that ticked has stopped,
And space stares, all around,
Or grisly frosts, first autumn morns,
Repeal the beating ground.

But most like chaos,—stopless, cool,—
Without a chance or spar,
Or even a report of land
To justify despair.

If you were coming in the fall,
I'd brush the summer by
With half a smile and half a spurn,
As housewives do a fly.

If I could see you in a year,
I'd wind the months in balls,
And put them each in separate drawers,
Until their time befalls.

If only centuries delayed,
I'd count them on my hand,
Subtracting till my fingers dropped
Into Van Diemen's land.

If certain, when this life was out,
That yours and mine, should be,
I'd toss it yonder, like a rind,
And taste eternity.

But now, uncertain of the length
Of time's uncertain wing,
It goads me, like the goblin bee,
That will not state its sting.

I like to see it lap the miles,
And lick the valleys up,
And stop to feed itself at tanks;
And then, prodigious, step

Around a pile of mountains,
And, supercilious, peer
In shanties by the sides of roads;
And then a quarry pare

To fit its sides, and crawl between,
Complaining all the while
In horrid hooting stanza;
Then chase itself down hill

And neigh like Boanerges;
Then, punctual as a star,
Stop—docile and omnipotent—
At its own stable door.

It makes no difference abroad,
The seasons fit the same,
The mornings blossom into noons,
And split their pods of flame.

Wild-flowers kindle in the woods,
The brooks brag all the day;
No blackbird bates his jargoning
For passing Calvary.

Auto-da-fé and judgment
Are nothing to the bee;
His separation from his rose
To him seems misery.

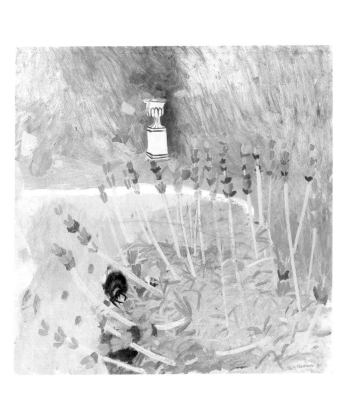

The brain is wider than the sky,
For, put them side by side,
The one the other will include
With ease, and you beside.

The brain is deeper than the sea,
For, hold them, blue to blue,
The one the other will absorb,
As sponges, buckets do.

The brain is just the weight of God,
For, lift them, pound for pound,
And they will differ, if they do,
As syllable from sound.

I've seen a dying eye
Run round and round a room
In search of something, as it seemed,
Then cloudier become;
And then, obscure with fog,
And then, be soldered down,
Without disclosing what it be,
'T were blessed to have seen.

I asked no other thing,
No other was denied.
I offered Being for it;
The mighty merchant smiled.

Brazil? He twirled a button,
Without a glance my way:
'But, madam, is there nothing else
That we can show to-day?'

Because I could not stop for Death,
He kindly stopped for me;
The carriage held but just ourselves
And Immortality.

We slowly drove, he knew no haste,
And I had put away
My labor, and my leisure too,
For his civility.

We passed the school where children played,
Their lessons scarcely done;
We passed the fields of gazing grain,
We passed the setting sun.

We paused before a house that seemed
A swelling of the ground;
The roof was scarcely visible,
The cornice but a mound.

Since then 't is centuries; but each
Feels shorter than the day
I first surmised the horses' heads
Were toward eternity.

I cannot live with you,
It would be life,
And life is over there
Behind the shelf

The sexton keeps the key to,
Putting up
Our life, his porcelain,
Like a cup

Discarded of the housewife,
Quaint or broken;
A newer Sèvres pleases,
Old ones crack.

I could not die with you,
For one must wait
To shut the other's gaze down,
You could not.

And I, could I stand by
And see you freeze,
Without my right of frost,
Death's privilege?

Nor could I rise with you,
Because your face
Would put out Jesus',
That new grace

Glow plain and foreign
On my homesick eye,

Except that you, than he
Shone closer by.

They'd judge us—how?
For you served heaven, you know,
Or sought to,
I could not,

Because you saturated sight,
And I had no more eyes
For sordid excellence
As Paradise.

And were you lost, I would be,
Though my name
Rang loudest
On the heavenly fame.

And were you saved,
And I condemned to be
Where you were not,
That self were hell to me.

So we must meet apart,
You there, I here,
With just the door ajar
That oceans are,
And prayer,
And that pale sustenance,
Despair!

A narrow fellow in the grass
Occasionally rides;
You may have met him,—did you not,
His notice sudden is.

The grass divides as with a comb,
A spotted shaft is seen;
And then it closes at your feet
And opens further on.

He likes a boggy acre,
A floor too cool for corn.
Yet when a child, and barefoot,
I more than once, at morn,

Have passed, I thought, a whip-lash
Unbraiding in the sun,—
When, stooping to secure it,
It wrinkled, and was gone.

Several of nature's people
I know and they know me;
I feel for them a transport
Of cordiality;

But never met this fellow,
Attended or alone,
Without a tighter breathing,
And zero at the bone.

I years had been from home,
And now, before the door,
I dared not open, lest a face
I never saw before

Stare vacant into mine
And ask my business there.
My business,—just a life I left,
Was such still dwelling there?

I fumbled at my nerve,
I scanned the windows near;
The silence like an ocean rolled,
And broke against my ear.

I laughed a wooden laugh
That I could fear a door,
Who danger and the dead had faced,
And never quaked before.

I fitted to the latch
My hand, with trembling care,
Lest back the awful door should spring,
And leave me standing there.

I moved my fingers off
As cautiously as glass,
And held my ears, and like a thief
Fled gasping from the house.

Ample make this bed.
Make this bed with awe;
In it wait till judgment break
Excellent and fair.

Be its mattress straight,
Be its pillow round;
Let no sunrise' yellow noise
Interrupt this ground.

      ❦❦❦

I felt a clearing in my mind
As if my brain had split;
I tried to match it, seam by seam,
But could not make them fit.

The thought behind I strove to join
Unto the thought before,
But sequence ravelled out of reach
Like balls upon a floor.

There came a wind like a bugle;
It quivered through the grass,
And a green chill upon the heat
So ominous did pass
We barred the windows and the doors
As from an emerald ghost;
The doom's electric moccason
That very instant passed.
On a strange mob of panting trees,
And fences fled away,
And rivers where the houses ran
The living looked that day.
The bell within the steeple wild
The flying tidings whirled.
How much can come
And much can go,
And yet abide the world!

I never saw a moor;
I never saw the sea;
Yet know I how the heather looks,
And what a wave must be.

I never spoke with God,
Nor visited in heaven;
Yet certain am I of the spot
As if the chart were given.

※※※

At half-past three a single bird
Unto a silent sky
Propounded but a single term
Of cautious melody.

At half-past four, experiment
Had subjugated test,
And lo! her silver principle
Supplanted all the rest.

At half-past seven, element
Nor implement was seen.
And place was where the presence was,
Circumference between.

The last night that she lived,
It was a common night,
Except the dying; this to us
Made nature different.

We noticed smallest things,—
Things overlooked before,
By this great light upon our minds
Italicized, as 't were.

That others could exist
While she must finish quite,
A jealousy for her arose
So nearly infinite.

We waited while she passed;
It was a narrow time,
Too jostled were our souls to speak,
At length the notice came.

She mentioned, and forgot;
Then lightly as a reed
Bent to the water, shivered scarce,
Consented, and was dead.

And we, we placed the hair,
And drew the head erect;
And then an awful leisure was,
Our faith to regulate.

We never know how high we are
Till we are called to rise;
And then, if we are true to plan,
Our statures touch the skies.

The heroism we recite
Would be a daily thing,
Did not ourselves the cubits warp
For fear to be a king.

My life closed twice before its close;
It yet remains to see
If Immortality unveil
A third event to me

So huge, so hopeless to conceive
As these that twice befell.
Parting is all we know of heaven,
And all we need of hell.

NOTES ON THE POEMS

Where there are differences between the actual words used by Emily Dickinson in the poems published in the Harvard variorum edition and those printed in this book, these are listed below. Discrepancies in punctuation and spelling are not noted.

p.21 1.5: Light laughs the breeze/In her Castle above them–

p.24 'I'm nobody! Who are you?' 1.4: Don't tell! they'd advertise–you know! 1.7: To tell one's name–the livelong June–

p.25 A fifth verse: And then a Plank in Reason, broke,/And I dropped down, and down–/And hit a World at every plunge,/And finished knowing–then–

p.26 1.3: That oppresses, like the Heft 1.9: None may teach it–Any–/'Tis the Seal Despair

p.28 1.3: On her divine Majority–/Present no more–

p.33 1.2: The Stillness in the Room 1.5: The Eyes around–had wrung them dry–/And Breaths were gathering firm 1.8: Be witnessed–in the Room– 1.10: What portion of me be/Assignable–and then it was

p.35 1.10: That hurried all around

p.36 1.7: 'And I–for Truth–Themself are One–

p.37 'The heart asks pleasure first' 1.8: The privilege to die–

p.40 1.8: For fear the numbers fuse– 1.16: And take Eternity– 1.18: Of this, that is between,

p.41 1.9: To fit its Ribs/And Crawl between

p.42 1.6: The Brooks slam–all the Day–/No Black bird bates his Banjo– 1.12: To Him–sums Misery–

p.44 1.3: The one the other will contain 1.10: For–Heft them–Pound for Pound–

p.45 'I asked no other thing' 1.4: The Mighty Merchant sneered–

p.47 1.9: We passed the School, where Children strove/At Recess in the Ring–/ A fourth verse: Or rather–He passed Us–/The Dews drew quivering and chill–/For only Gossamer, my Gown–/My Tippet–only Tulle– 1.16: The Cornice–in the Ground–/Since then–'tis Centuries–and yet

p.49 1.24: And that White Sustenance–

p.50 1.11: Yet when a Boy, and Barefoot–/I more than once at Noon

p.52 1.3: I dared not enter, lest a Face 1.5: Stare stolid into mine 1.7: My Business but a Life I left/Was such remaining there?'/I leaned upon the Awe–/I lingered with Before–/The Second like an Ocean rolled/And broke against my ear–/I laughed a crumbling Laugh/That I could fear a Door/Who Consternation compassed/And never winced before. 1.20: And leave me in the Floor–/Then moved my Fingers off

NOTES ON THE PICTURES

p.51 Mary Newcomb. *The Snake I Disturbed*, 1984. Oil on board. Private collection. Reproduced by permission of the artist. Photo: Crane Kalman Gallery, London.

p.55 Marsden Hartley (1877–1943). *Storm Clouds, Maine*, 1906–7. Oil on canvas. Collection Walker Art Center, Minneapolis. Gift of the T. B. Walker Foundation.

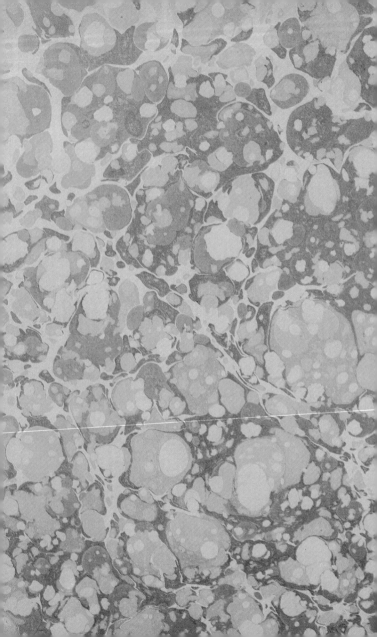